RED WALLS, BLACK HATS

An Amish Barn Raising

RED WALLS, BLACK HATS
An Amish Barn Raising

A photo essay by
Jim Weyer

Text by
Dick Roberts

Dedicated to the Amish people
who have struggled so valiantly
to maintain their way of life.

RED WALLS, BLACK HATS
An Amish Barn Raising

Copyright ©1988 by Jim Weyer

Published by
Weyer International
Book Division
(Formerly Knife Art Books Division,
Weyer Photo Services, Inc.)
333 14th St.
Toledo, OH 43624

Library of Congress
Catalog Card Number: 84-90471
ISBN: 0-9613834-3-7

Published November, 1988

20.00

Acknolwedgements

Reproduction photos printed on Ilford Multigrade FB
Design and Typography by Roy Meade
Printed on Cameo Dull Text
Equipment: Two Nikon bodies-20, 24, 35, 50, 105, 200 and 500mm lenses

Preface

There is a cruel irony about the objection of the Amish to cameras — an objection firmly based upon the Second Commandment's admonition that "thou shall not take unto thee any graven image."

The irony is this: simply because the "plain people" are so opposed to having their pictures taken, they make themselves more challenging to the hordes of tourists who invade their communities to point and stare.

The more elusive the prey, the more persistent and rude these visitors become, like hunters determined to carry home photographic trophies of the chase.

Anyone who makes any effort at all to understand the Amish — to appreciate the depth of their convictions and the reasons for their life-style — will find them a kind, gentle, peace-loving people. I learned fifteen years ago, when I first began taking pictures in Ohio's Holmes County, that if you treat the Amish with courtesy and respect they will respond in the same vein. But — I quickly realized — it is neither courteous nor respectful to ask them to pose for photographs.

I learned, too — during conversations with the Holmes County Amish community — that they have become philosophical about the subject, resigned to this intrusion into the privacy they cherish. One community elder, who became a friend, put it this way:

"What can we do about it? Nothing. We can try to ignore it, and that isn't always easy. If we're going about our business and people shoot pictures of us, we can't stop them. We'll simply continue what we're doing. But we resent being asked to stop and pose, and we won't."

In the ensuing years I have taken many pictures of the Amish — following the "ground rules" laid down by my friends in Holmes County — without ever becoming intrusive or disrespectful. I have had no complaints.

My experience has been quite the opposite, as illustrated by the pictures in this book. Many of them appeared in a corporate magazine.

Some of the men who appear on these pages asked if they might see the pictures, and carried home every one of the 200 copies of the magazine we distributed through their churches.

They didn't want the photos because they were in them, because vanity is as foreign to their makeup as pride and conceit. They wanted them for the same reason I had wanted to take them in the first place: they represent one facet of Amish life that is being seen less and less often today.

In many Amish communities throughout the country the one-day barn-raising like this has already become a thing of the past. Barns are being made of cement block, or sheet metal.

That's why the men who built the barn wanted pictures, even though they were shown in them: now they have something to show their grandchildren to remind them that — then as now — "love thy neighbor" has always been a foundation of Amish life.

Jim Weyer

Foreword

It is rare when one can be exposed to the works of a talented professional and a group of cultural craftsmen at the same sitting. This amazing book brings both together in a fascinating display.

Here, Jim Weyer, noted photo essayist, using the tool of his trade, a camera, focuses intimately into one facet of the Amish lifestyle.

After a review of this book, the reader will feel he or she has witnessed a personal, private and privileged look into an "age old custom"....an authentic Amish barn raising.

Amish barn raisings are rarely seen by non-Amish people. They are usually spontaneous and organized by a word-of-mouth communication between neighbors and friends. The "raising" is completed in old skillful ways, without fanfare.

Mr. Weyer through his masterful photography takes you page by page into this rare aspect of Amish life.

Modern societies have consumed most cultures or brought them into a mold to fit our fast-paced world. Only the Amish remain, making their past......their present.

As the Amish build their barn in this book, they will build admiration and respect in the eyes of the reader.

This wonderful display of love, cooperation and friendliness of the Amish are many of the important ingredients that make America....the beautiful.

It is our hope that this epic of Amish life, another highlight in Jim Weyer's long accomplished career, will bring you, the reader, a better understanding of these gentle folk.

Clyde S. Scoles

Clyde S. Scoles

Director of Toledo-Lucas County Library System

Introduction

Clyde Penrod and his wife Ruth waited, in the fog-shrouded early dawn, to see who would come down the country lane to their house.

They hoped a lot of people would come, even though Clyde and Ruth would know few of them personally and the people who might come down the lane would know even less about the Penrods, except for one thing:

They were neighbors, and they needed help. In Amish country, that's all you need to know.

Clyde grew up in Holmes County — in the rolling hills of Central Ohio that are home to the World's largest Amish community — and his earliest recollections are filled with the black buggies that busied the roads of his childhood.

He knew, as anyone must know who grows up among the "plain" people, that the Amish look after their own. They buy no life, health, or property insurance because they do not need it. They have no rest homes for the elderly because their elders are revered as patriarchs. They pay no Social Security taxes because of their refusal to accept Social Security benefits. "Our faith is sufficient to our needs," they testified, and Congress agreed.

Cradle to the grave security is something the Amish provide their people as a matter of faith. They are guided here, as in every aspect of their lives, by the Bible. And the Bible says (1 Timothy 5:8) "if any provide not for those of his house he hath denied the faith and is worse than an infidel."

Clyde and Ruth knew all this. After all, they had seen their neighbors swarming into the fields of those who were ill, or injured, or had died, putting in the crop. They had seen houses and barns rebuilt, in a day. They knew of neighbors whose hospital bills had been paid by the church. They had seen the "grosdaadi" houses adjoining the family homes, built for grandparents and great-grandparents. Finally, they had seen the long processions of black buggies carrying deceased friends to the cemeteries overlooking the valley — in plain coffins they had made for graves they had dug.

The Penrods knew all this. But they could not help recalling — as they awaited the dawn — that all those cases of brotherhood and compassion and kindness involved the Amish.

The injured, the sick, the aged, the deceased were all Amish. The people who came to their aid were Amish.

The Penrods were not. Would that matter?

That didn't mean the Penrods weren't known throughout their Sugar Creek community. The bearded men in the black buggies who waved as they passed knew a lot about Clyde — because the Amish are just as curious about their "English" neighbors as others are about the Amish.

They knew he was one of them — by occupation if not by religion — and that said a great deal about him. Labor is next to Godliness in the Amish faith, especially if it involves the soil. They knew Clyde milked a sizeable dairy herd, plowed the land, raised corn and oats, baled hay and did everything they did.

The Penrods were just as impressed by the industry and diligence of their Holmes County neighbors. They knew, particularly, how the Amish cherish and use every daylight hour — especially during the growing season — to plant and harvest their crops. Clyde and Ruth couldn't help wondering how many would be willing to give up this day for them.

As they waited for the first rays of the sun to burn through the fog that shrouded the valleys, the Penrods thought back to the day — nearly a month earlier — when they had crouched fearfully within the cement-block milking area as a tornado turned the barn above their heads into a swirling maelstrom of kindling.

They had just put their 17 holsteins and five jerseys into their stalls for the evening milking when Ruth — suddenly aware of a roaring noise — stepped outside to see what it was. She glanced up at the ridge that separates the Penrod farm from its nearest neighbor and saw a cloud of debris — the neighbor's barn — rising over the crest.

With all the unpredictability that makes this kind of storm so deadly, the tornado hop-skotched its way across Holmes County. It dipped to destroy the first barn, then leap-frogged the steep ridge and dipped once more, landing squarely atop the Penrod barn.

Inexplicably, the silo abutting the barn was not touched. Neither was the Penrod house, 200 feet away. The Penrods and their cows, sheltered by the cement-block milking area, were unharmed.

The barn was scattered across the countryside. The hillside over which the storm passed was carpeted with slate from the roof. The gauge Clyde uses to measure the quantity of milk in his holding tank was found a mile and a half away.

Time had dulled the terror of that moment, but what happened next was still sharp in their minds.

The dust had hardly settled, Clyde recalls, when the first black buggy came down the lane. They didn't know the driver, but that didn't surprise them. Were they all right? Assured that they were, the visitor left — to check on other homes. Later there were other buggies, other concerned queries about their safety.

And the following day Levi Erb came by.

Levi introduced himself and asked, "Do you want a new barn?"

That was a rhetorical question and Levi knew it. When winter comes, Clyde brings his herd into their stalls and they stay there until spring. During those winter months he must have storage space for their hay and grain, the straw for their beds, and machinery.

Clyde told Levi that he certainly did want a new barn.

Nobody keeps track of these things, but if they did Levi Erb would certainly emerge as king of the barn builders. He has lost track of the numbers, but Levi and his crew have become modern-day legends among the Amish.

Clyde recalls what happened next; "He spent the entire day, sitting under that oak tree up there on the bank, just figuring."

Levi had done this a hundred times before, but he didn't earn his reputation by guesswork. His "figuring" involved a precise listing of every eight-by-eight (timbers eight inches square), every four-by-four, every two-by-six needed to frame a building 66 feet long, 36 wide, and 50 feet high.

When he was done, Levi went to Clyde's wood-lot and marked the trees that would yield the required timbers — forty and fifty-foot oaks — and a cutting crew came in, felled the trees, and hauled them to the sawmill.

But Levi wasn't the only visitor the day after the tornado. Lewis Schlabach, an Amishman whose farm abuts Clyde's, stopped by. A dairy farmer himself, he had recently sold his herd and knew something about cows that most people don't:

You can't just _not_ milk them. If you don't, they lose their milk and dry up. Lewis knew Clyde had to do something quickly about his herd, and he had a suggestion: "Bring them over to my place," he offered. "I've got plenty of pasture and everything you need is right there in the barn."

Relieved but not surpised, Clyde accepted gratefully. For the next 23 days the Schlabach fields and barn were home to the Penrod herd.

Levi Erb and his crew, meanwhile, were busy. Their work had just begun when the big timbers arrived from the sawmill.

There have been no changes, in the past 350 years, in the way the Amish build their barns. As in everything they do, simplicity is the rule.

The Amish barn gets its strength and stability from three simple techniques — the mortise, tenon, and wooden peg.

The mortise is a rectangular recess cut into the upright eight-by-eights. You start with the auger holes, then shape them with hammer and chisel. The tenon is a tongue fashioned on the ends of the cross-timbers. They have to fit perfectly within the mortises. Holes are bored through both mortise and tenon, and foot-long wooden pegs driven through them to lock them in place.

Amish farming is perhaps the most labor-intensive on earth, but large families (10 and 12 children aren't unusual) make light work of heavy chores. Raising a barn may be heavier work than anything the farmer encounters at home — but there are many, many more hands.

There were soon enough strong arms for the job, and before the first rays of the morning sun broke through fifty pairs of them had seized the first of the massive sections — weighing several tons — and lifted it from the floor.

When it had been lifted as far as arms could reach, other men with long, spike-tipped poles pushed it higher. Men with ropes, meanwhile, helped pull the section upright and anchored it in place until it could be connected to the rest of the frame.

As each successive section was raised into place, tenons slid into mortises, the wooden pegs locked them firmly together, and soon the frame was almost completed. Nobody was at all surprised that everything fitted perfectly, and that Levi Erb and his men had cut, trimmed, shaped, bored and chiseled one more clockwork, picture-perfect barn.

Even as one group climbed atop the frame to begin raising the roof rafters, another swarmed around the foundation nailing on the siding. As soon as one section of rafters was in place, dozens of men converged on it like ants to hammer down the sheet-iron roofing.

By four o'clock in the afternoon, ten hours after the first mist-muffled buggy came down the lane, Clyde and Ruth Penrod had a new barn.

The whole experience, mind-boggling to Clyde and Ruth, was rather ho-hum to their new friends, who are accustomed to doing things together and enjoy it immensely. A barn-raising, like a horse auction or farm sale, gives them a welcome opportunity to visit, to exchange news, discuss church and personal business — to talk about crops and horses and the things they all do every day.

And while the men worked on the barn, the women and girls were in the Penrod house preparing a typically abundant Amish meal — plain but plentiful — drawn from the bounty of garden and field. Mealtime, too, is a cherished opportunity for visiting.

Clyde has no idea how many came to help, although he guesses there must have been somewhere around 250. They weren't all there at the same time: some came early and left at noon or soon after because they had work to do at home, and others came later after spending part of the day in the fields.

Many of his benefactors, Clyde knew, he might never see again because they came from outside Holmes County. He wanted to thank them all, while they were there giving him one of their most precious gifts — their time — but didn't. It would have embarassed them, he sensed, knowing that the Amish feel about public expression of sentiment the way they feel about flashy clothes.

Instead, he paid for a small "Thank you" ad in The Budget, whose masthead describes itself as "A Weekly Newspaper Serving the Sugarcreek Area and Amish-Mennonite Communities throughout the Americas."

The Budget is filled with the comings and goings of the Amish wherever they live — the births, deaths, weddings, who-visited-whom — an unending compendium of personals that are avidly followed by its readers.

His low-key, subdued expression of appreciation in that newspaper, Clyde admits now, was the best way possible to convey his feelings. "I realize now that they didn't expect any more than that," he says — adding, "I don't think they expected anything at all."

If he didn't know it before the tornado, he certainly knows it now: labor is a manifestation of the faith that binds them together and impels them to come to the aid of any neighbor in need.

"And you don't have to be Amish," Clyde says. "Thank God for neighbors like these."

Dick Roberts

Dick Roberts

5:52 AM.....
The first buggy arrives...

The Horses

One of the first things the tourist notices — after the black buggies — are the horses pulling them.

They look like racehorses and there's a very good reason why they should: virtually all of them come from Eastern harness-racing tracks. Too old to race, or not quite good enough to make the winner's circle, they are usually picked up at the tracks by brokers who truck them back to Amish communities to be sold at auction.

Here as at the farm sales where antique dealers bid up the price of hand tools, household implements, and other Amish memorabilia, the Amish are forced into bidding contests with buyers who ship them to Europe and elsewhere.

They are either pacers or trotters, with mile-eating gaits that carry them effortless along the rural highways in Amish communities. They can cover perhaps 10 miles in an hour, but after 20 miles must be rested.

That's a snail's pace, compared with the automobile, a fact brought up often by tourists who ask community members why they stick with the horse. They are especially curious in Holmes County, Ohio, the world's largest Amish community.

"Why, there's no way you can get to Cleveland, or Columbus, or Cincinnati," one inquisitor said to an elderly Amishman. "We know," he replied, smiling as if some private joke, "we know."

Pictures

*The Second Commandment says
"thou shall not make unto thee any
graven image, or any likeness of
anything that is in Heaven above,
or that is in the earth beneath, or
that is in the water under the
earth." (Exodus 20:4).*

Color in Amish Life

The Amish dress code reflects a rigid adherence to beliefs that clothing must embody the simplicity and modesty that governs their lives.

Men wear dark suits, coats without lapels, suspenders, broadfall pants with buttons instead of zippers, white or plain pastel shirts, black shoes, black or straw broad-rimmed hats. Beards are worn and the hair is worn full, trimmed at the collar line.

Women's and girl's dresses have full skirts, long sleeves, high necklines, with aprons and white "prayer veiling" covering the back and top of the head. Clothing is strictly functional: it covers the body, and protects it from sun and the rain.

The same strict rules apply to the home: everything there must serve a useful purpose.

But Amish women, who like pretty things as much as women anywhere in the world, have quietly worked a small miracle in their homes by equating "must serve" with "must have served."

Take, for example, the picture postcard. The Amish like to travel, and when they do they send back lots of beautiful scenic cards to their friends. These have a way of ending up on living room walls — and so what if they've been there four or five years? They served a useful purpose, didn't they?

And calendars — especially those with pretty scenes on them. What if they <u>were</u> several years old — they were useful and functional once.

And what woman can resist beautiful scenic and portrait plates lined up in her China cabinet? Just for show? Not at all. When guests show up and extra plates are needed these come down off the shelf and are heaped with typical Amish generosity. In other words, they are useful.

The very "plainness" of the Amish woman's dress can in itself be extraordinarily beautiful. Skirts must be of solid colors, but superimpose their intense purples, greens, grays, blues and browns against the somber backdrop of their men at a wedding — for example — and you have a pleasant mosaic of quiet and peaceful beauty.

There is nothing "drab" about the Amish home, a misconception spread by people who judge the Amish by their outward-lifestyle. There are flowers around the house and in among the vegetables in the garden, too, but the most attractive contribution the Amish women makes to brightening her home is in her needlework.

Her pillowcases, coverlets and bedspreads permit her to express her love of symmetry and beauty to the fullest. But her quilts, intricately, lovingly and painstakingly stitched together, make her the most sought-after "folk-artist" of our times.

They are far and away the most beautiful examples of their kind in America, and tourists carry them home by the thousands. The Amish, meanwhile, are pleased by this welcome income.

Their quilts, the Amish women say, are very useful and functional. They keep you warm at night. So what if they happen to be beautiful, too?

Why Not Cars?

Why do the Amish cling to their black buggies, certainly the most outdated and antiquated form of transportation in the country?

Is it simply because the buggy was good enough for their grandfathers and great-grandfathers, and so must be good enough for them? If that were the only reason it would be reason enough, in view of their determination to follow centuries-old practices, but it's only part of the answer.

The buggy is slow. The average horse can pull one perhaps 10 miles an hour, but after 20 miles or so must rest for several hours. This means the driver must reach a fellow-Amishman's home, where he knows he will be welcome.

Because of these limitations of time and distance, the buggy will not carry its driver to distant cities where "wicked" life-styles might tempt him. He is largely restricted to his community and that's the way he wants it — because the tightly-knit community ranks nearly as high as the tightly-knit family in the Amish way of life.

They noted, too, that the car has become a status symbol among their non-Amish neighbors, and that more expensive automobiles promoted class distinctions by indicating levels of wealth.

Amish buggies avoid this. They are so nearly alike that there is no way invidious comparisons can be made about their drivers.

Besides, the Amish are fond of saying, "the horse reproduces itself, but the automobile produces nothing but debt and expense."

"Secret" meetings

In the early 1500's, when both church and state were doing their utmost to wipe out the new faith growing up in Switzerland, the Amish were forced — as a matter of personal and religious survival — to meet secretly for worship.

They developed the practice of meeting in their own homes, choosing a different place each week.

That practice has endured to this day, although there is certainly no need for secrecy now. The "bench wagon," resembling a horse-drawn hearse, indicates where services are being held on any given Sunday. It delivers the hard, backless benches upon which worshippers sit during services that usually last at least four hours.

While the Amish now enjoy the freedom all religions in this country enjoy today, they are never going to forget — or let their children forget — the years of persecution that finally drove them from Europe.

The Bible and the Ausbund, one of the oldest of Protestant hymnals, will be found in every Old Order Amish home. And so will a third book — The Martyr's Mirror.

The Mirror, nearly a thousand pages long, chronicles the suffering and death from torture, execution and harrassment, endured by the founders of their faith who had no freedom at all.

*Differences between Mennonite
and Amish*

More than 90 different kinds of buggies will be found in and around Amish communities in the United States.

There are many obvious differences among them: there are open one-seaters and two-seaters, closed one-seaters and two-seaters, and racy two-wheelers that look like the sulkies that circle America's harness-racing tracks.

But they all seem to be driven by bearded men in dark clothes and wide-brimmed hats and so the casual observer concludes they are all Amish and all alike.

Nothing could be farther from the truth. First, the bearded drivers may be Mennonite, not Amish. Second, even if they were all Amish they would differ from one another in a hundred ways that are as obvious as day and night to the Amish but unintelligible to the tourist.

The Mennonites and Amish trace their roots back to Fifteenth Century Switzerland where they were persecuted, tortured, killed and finally driven from the country. The Mennonites split from the Amish not because of differences in faith, but in their interpretation of how far Christianity should go in accommodating modern progress.

They permit no personal adornment. Many will not even paint their houses. They use buttons and safety pins instead of zippers, horses in the fields, and have no telephones or electricity in the home.

Everything in the home must be functional and useful, and nothing is there because it is just decorative or pretty. Plain window blinds, for example, are just as functional as drapes.

The Mennonites, as tenacious in their religious beliefs as the Amish, nonetheless feel that their interpretation of the Bible permits latitude that the Amish can never accept.

They may drive cars, and use tractors in the fields. Their homes have electricity and telephones and TV. They favor higher education — while the Amish limit the formal education of their children to the eighth grade. They enter professions that the Amish shun.

And many of them still dress like the Amish, adding to the confusion. They live in the same communities, but worship separately — the Amish in their own homes and the Mennonites in churches and meeting houses.

Moreover, the Amish — for all their seeming uniformity (black clothes, beards, broad-rimmed hats) are as diverse a group as one will find anywhere.

Any one of a hundred variations of transport, dress, or life-style may indicate a subtle difference in Bible interpretation. Take the ubiquitous black buggy, for example.

Perhaps they all look alike, to the tourist, but: are they rubber-tired, or steel rimmed? What about the windows — how big are they? Do they have the standard triangular slow-moving-vehicle emblem on the back — or reflective tape? How about battery-operated head and tail lights? Is the top black — or white, brown, or yellow? Does it have a storm front? Does it have sliding doors, or roll-down curtains? Is there a whip socket? And are the sides angled, or straight?

Each subtle difference indicates that the driver belongs to a particular church congregation, because each church sets its own rules about how its members will dress, travel, work and live.

The Amish are not in the least concerned because their "English" neighbors cannot detect these obscure nuances of religion. It is enough that they understand them, and accept them. Whether you prefer steel-rimmed or rubber-tired buggies, you are still Amish. And if your church mandates rubber tires, but you consider them vain and ostentatious, you can switch to a congregation that agrees with you.

Non-conformity, after all, is the basis of their faith — even if it involves non-conformity with each other. The Bible speaks plainly on the subject:

"Come out from among them, and be ye separate," it says in 2 Corinthians 6:17. And Romans 12:2 warns, "be not conformed to this world."

Schools

Formal education of Amish children ends with the eighth grade.

Too much education, their parents feel, would make them too worldly. Besides, public high schools stress material the Amish child will never use: why, for example, teach science to the boy who will devote his life to the soil — or the girl who will become housewife and mother?

The "plain people" endured years of legal pressure and occasionally imprisonment before the highest court in the land exempted Amish children from compulsory attendance beyond the elementary grades.

While some formal education is important, the Amish feel, it is not nearly as essential to their children as the continuing education they receive in home and church — education that stresses the life-styles, beliefs, and religious convictions of the parents.

Four years of high school, the Amish feel, would deprive their children of their most valuable learning years — when the boys are in the fields with their fathers and the girls in the homes with their mothers.

The home becomes a closely-knit, loving, familial vocational institute where children learn by watching, imitation and instruction, gradually moving from one assigned task to a more difficult one until they have mastered the skills of agriculture and home-making and absorbed their unique cultural and religious heritage.

The one-room schoolhouse, usually taught by an Amish woman who herself has no more than an eighth grade education, is the mainstay of the Amish educational system. They build and maintain their own schools and print their own textbooks.

Their children, the Amish will tell anyone who asks, are not learning basic skills in their schools — but basic values.

Chief Justice Warren Burger of the Supreme Court sustained this distinction when he ruled, in 1972, that "it is neither fair nor correct to suggest that the Amish are opposed to education beyond the eighth grade level. What the record shows is that they are opposed to conventional formal education of the type provided by certified high schools because it comes at the child's crucial adolescent period of religious development."

Jobs

There will never be enough land for all the young men who grow up in all the large families the Amish typically rear — which means they must find employment "outside."

Despite this, they stay as close to their roots as they can — working in jobs that provide goods and services for their communities or which use the products of Amish farms.

Cheesemaking is an example. Because the Amish have traditionally lacked the electricity to cool their milk, they have had to dispose of it quickly. In response to this need, many small cheesemaking plants have sprung up in and around their communities.

Many others find work in timber-related fields like lumbering, in sawmills, and especially in wood-working. The Amish are skilled carpenters, and are sought-after for buggy, furniture, and cabinet-making, and in mobile home production.

Some are self-employed as builders, blacksmiths, harness-makers, printers, clockmakers, butchers and in feed mills and dairies. But there are many professions the Amish will not enter, because they are too "worldly."

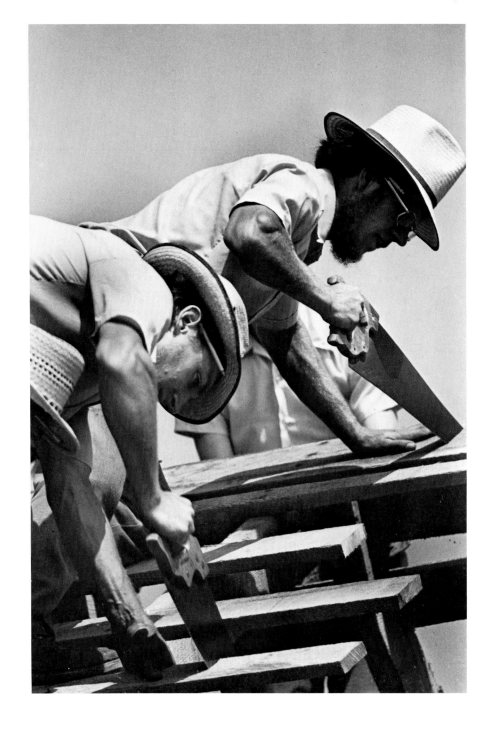

Can They Survive?

Can the Amish survive the ever-increasing technological and social pressure that they face?

Can they maintain their "plain" way of life — their lives of simplicity, faith and non-conformity — in a world that considers them anachronisms, culturally mired in the past and out of step with the present?

If they felt the slightest compulsion to explain themselves to their "English" neighbors — and they don't — the Amish themselves might point out that they *have* changed, very slowly but still steadily, over the past two decades. These changes, so subtle that the casual observer might not see them at all, are significant to the Amish and are being made only after long soul-searching and prayer.

Circumstances have forced some of these changes upon them. Take, for example, the use of horse-powered equipment in the fields — long the most visible symbol of the Amish farm.

The big farm equipment manufacturers, mindful of demands for mechanization, long ago stopped making the horse-drawn reapers, the McCormick mowers, the hay rakes and plows the Amish have depended upon. They have been patched and mended and re-built until there isn't much left.

Now, frequently, tractors will be found in Amish barnyards. They are usually parked there and used only for power take-off — providing belt power for chopping corn and filling silos. They are always steel-tired, because pneumatic tires are forbidden by the Old Order Amish.

Occasionally, but still rarely, tractors will be seen pulling equipment in the field. Gasoline or diesel engines are being hauled into the field (by horses) to provide power there. The Amish are beginning to use some electricity in their homes if they produce it themselves, and gasoline engines are being used to operate refrigerators and milk coolers.

Scarcity of land in and around their communities, and the spiralling cost of land, are forcing other changes in the Amish way of life. More and more of their young are being forced into jobs not related to farming. Some — perhaps one out of ten — are "cutting their hair" and leaving the faith for the outside world.

Taxes pose an ever-increasing threat to an Amish economy already burdened by taxes. The Amish educate their own children, provide their own teachers and textbooks, providing land and lumber for school buildings. But they must still pay school taxes for children other than their own. As "English" population grows in their communities, as more and more schools are built for their education, taxes on Amish farms become more burdensome.

These changes — technological, sociological, governmental — are among the most serious threats to the Amish way of life.

Sociologists forty years ago decided that the Amish culture could not possibly survive the pressures of modern civilization. They aren't nearly as certain about that now. They admit that they underestimated the strength of Amish faith, the determination — forged on centuries of persecution — to follow their own path.

Now they conclude that — with gradual adaptation to the "outside" world — the Amish will indeed survive. It is unfortunate that sociologists must base so many of their conclusions on such things as abstract data and census figures.

It is doubtful if any of them ever read this:

> "Oh my dearest love on earth, kiss all my children once for me, and tell my Susan that it is her father's wish that she be obedient to her mother in the fear of God."

That is a passage from _The Martyr's Mirror,_ the thousand-page compendium of torture and death found in most Old Order Amish homes. It was written by a father who was about to die rather than recant his faith — one of the thousands who suffered and died for their beliefs 300 years ago.

It is not likely that a culture that has survived so much will lose its identity merely because its followers may one day have to use tractors in the fields.

As America's Amish population continues its steady growth, pressures to find land for the newcomers grows right along with it.

Given the choice, every Amishman would own and work a farm. Tilling the soil is a God-ordained thing with them — one of the foundations upon which their religion and tradition rests.

But as their numbers grow, the land available to them dwindles and becomes increasingly costly. The farm traditionally passes from father to son, which means that very little of it ever comes up for sale. Larger farms have been subdivided, in past decades, to provide land for children and others, so that most Amish farms have been reduced to the bare minimums needed to support large families.

Much of the land has been in the family for generations, and is not encumbered by debt. It was paid for years ago — and Amish farms escaped the foreclosures that wiped out thousands of debt-burdened family farms in the 1980's.

Those who are determined to farm, but cannot find land in their own communities, may move on. New communities are being established across the country, with one, two, or three families forming nuclei around which others will form new settlements. In the past year, two new communities have been established in Texas and one in Michigan.

The Amish now have settlements in 19 states and Canada. Their largest presence is in Ohio, especially in Holmes County, the largest Amish community in the world. But only half of Ohio's "plain people" are now farming.

Growth of Amish religion

The Old Order Amish represent the fastest-growing religion in the country. Their numbers, currently estimated around 100,000, have doubled since 1970 and show no signs of abating.

One obvious reason for this growth, of course, are the large families typically found on the Amish farm which average between seven and eight children and often number 10 or more.

Amish children are nurtured and loved perhaps more warmly than children anywhere on earth, growing up with the certainty that their every need from cradle to the grave will be provided by family, community, and church. Divorce and separation are virtually unheard of, and Amish family cohesiveness is unmatched anywhere.

Large families are a necessity on the Amish farm, which is enormously labor-intensive, depending upon the skills and strength of many hands to take the place of electricity and machinery.

These two factors — the need for many helping hands and an innate love of children — might be explanation enough for the dramatic growth of the religion, but they are only part of the answer.

As in everything they do, the Amish heed the words of the Bible, including the admonition in Psalms 127:3 reminding them that "children are the heritage of the Lord and the fruit of the womb is His reward."